MY BROTHER'S SHOT

MY BROTHER'S SHOT

The Boy to Man Handbook
for Navigating the Teen Years

Y.R. SPENCE

My Brother's Shot
The Boy to Man Handbook for Navigating the Teen Years

Copyright © 2021 Y.R. Spence

All rights reserved. No part of this publication may be reproduced, distributed, or transmitted in any form or by any means, including photocopying, recording, or other electronic or mechanical methods, without the prior written permission of the publisher, except in the case of brief quotations embodied in critical reviews and certain other noncommercial uses permitted by copyright law.

Y.R. Spence
Houston, TX

In association with
Elite Online Publishing
63 East 11400 South Suite #230
Sandy, UT 84070
EliteOnlinePublishing.com

Editor: Eileen Ansel Conery, APR
Book Designer: Michelle M. White

Printed in the United States of America

ISBN: 978-1513676999

Contents

Introduction	1
Accountability of the Black Man	9
Advice Statements	13
Education / Employment	17
Family	25
Tommy at Breakfast	35
Friends	39
Character	43
Satan My Friend	59
Love and Romance	63
Finance	71
Loyalty	79
Food	83
Faith	89
Know This…	93
Government / World History	97
Success	103
Quotes from the Heart	109
Health & Hygiene	113
Home Life	119
I'm a Proud Black Man	127
Travel	131
Entertainment	137
Being a Man is Being a Dad	141
Bible Verses	145
My Brother's Shot	153
About the Author	159

Introduction

INTRODUCTION

As a father to young adult children, as well as a lifestyle and relationship coach, I've thought for years about creating a guidebook to help those most vulnerable within our community, mainly the young man of color who might not have the advantage of consistent, loving guidance in his life. My Brother's Shot is a book geared towards bringing awareness to the challenges faced by African American men, as well as other men of color in our country. These challenges are found within all rooms: the board room, classroom, courtroom, and bedroom. There's a destructive breakdown in society where the role of the black man has been, and continues to be, diminished. The word "man" has become a noun only, the adjective "man" is a mischaracterization of a chauvinistic pig that only wants women barefoot and pregnant, cooking in the kitchen for the ones who stick around. Our men often are seen as sagging pants, drug-dealing criminals. Does this sound familiar? I'm referring to that brother who is ready to abandon his family in pursuit of that rap career?

The rap career that takes him to late-night hangouts, drinking and smoking, but since it's at a studio it's considered work. The brothers claim they're boss, because they sell drugs and belittle the men that wake up at 6 a.m. to go to work. Not realizing that the work money soon could be much-needed bail money. You know those brothers who make fun of the friend that went to college calling him "Hey Joe College" not understanding that in the years to come they'll want that same person to be their son's Godfather, as well as the guy to whom they turn when their pockets are low in cash. Somehow, we need to dispel the belief that we don't need education to be successful. Asking instead, what kind of education does one need in order to be successful? Education comes in many different forms and places: the classroom, traveling, life experiences. There are millions of people who went to some of the top law, medical, or engineering schools. There are even more who attended the School of Hard Knocks. Whether it's an advanced degree or a fourth grade education, what separates one by the age of 40 is one's drive, passion, and will to succeed. By finding one's passion and developing the drive, anyone can succeed at any task. So, contemplate: what's your passion and what would you do if money wasn't an issue?

Then the drive: what are you willing to do better and what are you willing to give up in order to obtain your goals? The ultimate question is how much are you able to commit to working? Work on your targeted obsessive goal. Allow it to consume you until your dream consumes others.

Today, the hard part is that the ones who are supposed to be there to protect and serve are disproportionately killing our men of color. As much as their deeds are wicked and it shows us who they are, we need to understand who we are. If one of our own gets shot, we all get shot. If one's knee is on our neck, that knee is on all our necks.

Only the names change. At the point of death, the causality goes out the window. Always pay attention to the ones who ask, what did he do. Those are the ones who will try to justify the killing, the murder. Those are the ones who are building a case to defend the killer. By ignoring it or simply walking away from it, it will leave more of an impression than an actual conversation. The conversation will not go well since it would be arguing from a place of emotion, whereas this group has had years to practice its defense.

We live in a society that is desperately seeking strong male role models, but far too often these men are rejected by the people who need them the most.

Culturally, the word father is being replaced as a norm by the term baby daddy. Industries, such as the mattress industry in particular have grown in every corner of society, yet now caters to the single-parent household, which has sadly replaced the dual-parent household. Developers are building apartment buildings more and more to accommodate the single, unattached I-don't-need-to-commit-to-society type of resident.

We've become increasingly accepting of the lack of accountability and commitment, which sometimes comes from top leadership within our own Government. The most important words in America, along with the family unit, business relationships, friend relationships, all start with Love, Accountability, and Commitment (LAC). Love is an undetermined and consistently evolving word. The meaning changes from person to person, environment to environment, culture to culture, and man to woman. My focus starts with the love for one's own, whoever that might be. How we show love is self-determining and truly that's the inconsistency within our society, which at the root, at our core, is the beginning of the breakdown of our social construct. Controversially, there must be some consistencies in the way we show love to one another. It is paramount to observe and adopt loving behaviors, as well as to identify hateful and harmful behaviors. Usually, such concepts and behaviors are easy to find, yet difficult to fulfill, but why? Understand that love is a shared ideology to be shared among family, friends, and people one meets daily. The key phase is that love is meant to be shared. Since humans are selfish by nature, it is all the more difficult to show love for all. The belief that people can only love those who look like them, dress like them, eat the same food, and think as they do, is a thought process shared by closed-minded bigots and the beginning of shared racist ideals. Once the concept of one love, one blood is shared and agreed upon by all, the racial inequality will lessen.

The cause of the nuclear family breakdown is when we continue to build and accept the me first lifestyle. Knowing this, we will continue to see broken homes and broken families. You might ask how this happened when we love our family? One example is of the boys getting together to watch the big fight. The wife has a massive migraine headache and has retreated to her room while the kids play in their rooms unsupervised. At this point somehow you've convinced yourself that it's ok to leave the most important people in your life, your wife and kids, while your wife suffers and is incapable of overseeing the safety of the kids.

Second, the money you'll spend while out with the boys could pay for your children's school lunch for a week. Then there are the officers flashing those lights in your rear-view mirror, ever hear of DWI. This scenario is a stretch, yet one can fill in the details. My point is that it's hard to prioritize the importance of one's actions whenever selfish desires take hold. To whom are we showing love when we take illegal drugs, and to whom are we showing hate? I've yet to receive a solid response to this question. If we believe that we're consistently in a state of action or being. Is one's behavior reflecting a state of being when one is patrolling the boundaries to love or hate?

My brothers, read this book as a one-sided advising tool to aid in the growth and development of young African Americans, as well as any male of color. Sure, anyone can read this book, however the relevant audience is not aimed at the privileged schoolgirl with a 97 percent high school average, deciding between Harvard and Yale, and going to her home where both parents are present. It can be embraced by the average fatherless white teenager who's never been supported by stable adults. While reading, think about the mentor for that guy whom you've admired from afar? Picture him sitting you down and sharing these words of wisdom. Only by making it a real person, will they have the desired effect.

So, enjoy my personal life lessons, and those of my life-coaching clients as I address my people. This book isn't meant to simply be read once, but more of a reference guide to help one become the best person possible, even if that person isn't yet aware of how great they can become.

I thought it important to share that the title, My Brother's Shot, is multifaceted, as you'll see throughout the book. As you read, you'll begin to understand why I chose My Brother's Shot as the title of my book. Enjoy and have a happy, healthy life!

Accountability of the Black Man

Shall I run, not walk, to defend my brother? Shall I absorb the treatment of my brother? I am here for my brother. If it's done to him, it is done to me. I am here for my brother. If it's done to him, it's done to me.

If he riots, I riot. If he peacefully protests, we all should peacefully protest. Does his riot resemble my riot? Does his assembling methods coincide with mine? Most likely not, however, togetherness bonds us.

We are asked to forget about the lynching of the 1920s when they show pride and call those times the roaring 20s, when all was good in America. Did the lynching make us great or was it the overcoming of those brutal acts that have made us the shining beacon on the hill?

We read about the 1940s when President Truman showed courage and American's pound their chest for his actions in Hiroshima. However, these are people, too. Would we have felt the same if it were us and it was Boston? Would the narrative reflect the actions of a coward?

We're great people, however, we are comfortable falling behind all other races, cultures, and nationalities.

Killing each other doesn't make the news to the point that we defend killing each other as a way of life. We kill each other and justify it, but riot when it comes to the hand of the white man, a white policeman. Are we holding them to a higher standard? If so, why are they better than you or than us?

Are they correct? Are we savages by definition? Are we unable to control our actions or emotions? Are we cruel and vicious?

Do we positively enhance one another or do we make it more difficult for one another?

Do we reach back and help our brothers? Or, have we gotten bitten too many times for doing just that and therefore wrote off all other brothers needing a helping hand?

How do you get our brother going, our fathers staying, and our brothers working?

Yes, I am my brother's keeper, but is he mine? Does he expect excellence for himself as much as I do for him, I ask? I am my brother's keeper, but is he mine?

Have we accepted negative behavior as what's expected as normal?

Are we holding our brothers accountable as men or as savages?

Advice Statements

ADVICE STATEMENTS

For years I've thought about sharing tiny bits of advice that I have found to be useful in today's broken society. I've compiled these thoughts and quotes to help guide our most vulnerable in society, our young men of color with little to no guidance.

Please read each entry thoughtfully and reflect on the message. Take notes in the margins, share these ideas with loved ones, and add your own. Divided into life categories, you can refer back to the category at different moments as needed to hopefully help you navigate through any challenging situation.

Education / Employment

The transition between the end of education and the beginning of a professional work life can be a challenge. It could be just a bit easier for young people if they had guidance from more seasoned workers. In fact, many who begin a working life while still in high school also can most definitely benefit from advice. The contacts made in a person's first few jobs lead to bigger and better opportunities, often they are called upon for positive character recommendations for future jobs. Also, don't think that learning stops when school ends. Learning is endless and enriching.

Remember, no matter what people say, not everyone is supposed to go to college, learn a trade. Start early and you'll grow enormously successful.

Encourage the people you care about to pursue a higher level of education. Don't walk away, RUN from the person who doesn't support your education.

Give your employer your best every day, your efforts will be appreciated, but if not, you're with the wrong employer.

Take one college course at a major university on a subject in which you're interested. When looking for a job you'll always be able to put this experience on your resume, plus it just might help you professionally.

EDUCATION / EMPLOYMENT

Subscribe to your industry's newsletter or journal. The general knowledge you'll develop will be noticed, if applied correctly.

If you play sports in high school, the objective is to get a scholarship. Free education is priceless, focus on division two or three schools as a safe bet school.

Seek employment and housing at least 75 to 100 miles from where you grew up. Years from now you'll keep favorable memories of your youth and wish to return easily to your hometown.

Thoughts

Read the writings of Maya Angelou, then share her wisdom with others.

If you're not exploring college or a trade school, study your African American history.

Get involved with police department volunteer programs. This will be valuable, very valuable. You'll thank me the next time you get stopped or need assistance.

If your ambition is to become a rapper or professional athlete, great! Go for it with all you have! However, a solid education is a good back-up plan.

The average per-credit class at a university costs less than your Jordans. Check it out: average per credit class is $150, average cost for Air Jordan 5 retro goes for $180.

Volunteer at a fire department during Thanksgiving. Seeing those less fortunate in your area will give you a greater appreciation of what you have.

Watch 60 minutes of informative videos regularly. The knowledge you'll gain will allow you to get engaged in any conversation intellectually with most people.

Develop an in-depth knowledge of the successes and failures of the President(s) that you prefer.

Thoughts

At least once a year, visit your local library to observe people of all ages learning.

Know the differences between all units of the military and show respect.

Read an inspirational article in the magazine ESPN about someone you admire.

Read articles inconsistent with what you believe. It will always make you a better debater when you know the key points of the other side.

Understand when you're working hard, yet not smart. Employing technology would generate smart working habits most of the time.

EDUCATION / EMPLOYMENT

Open at least one part- or full-time business in your lifetime. You'll learn to appreciate the challenges of a small business owner.

Using the dictionary, as well as multiple other sources to learn the difference between a racist and a bigot.

When given an opportunity to learn something new or deepen your knowledge base, take it. Your education is one thing that no one can ever take away from you.

Thoughts

After reading this entry, stop and search YouTube for any speech by Dr. Claud Anderson, especially his speech regarding PowerNomics. You'll never be the same.

Download Wolfgang Riebe's 100 Quotations to Make You Think! It's free. In your downtime, it'll be a better alternative to Candy Crush or Mobile Strike.

Read the bio of Malcolm X or watch the movie directed by Spike Lee. All African Americans should understand his life and his death.

There's nothing wrong with not knowing. There's something wrong with not searching for the answers, however.

Family

Maintaining a healthy family connection is one of the keys to a happy life. Family bonds are tested through life's challenges, but a strong family bond can provide support and love to help make those challenging times easier to navigate. Nourish these connections and the benefits will come back tenfold.

Smile and kiss the first person you see as you walk into your house.

Know the difference between a house and a home, make sure you are instrumental in creating a home.

Learn from your father's or mentor's experiences, the conversation alone inspires you well.

Drive as if your grandma is in the passenger seat, with your mother seated behind you.

Spend time researching your last name and your family crest, if you have one.

Keep in touch with family members who are considered the "black sheep" or less driven.

Call your parents and kiss your kids. The way your children see you interact with your parents is the way they'll treat you in your old age.

Teach your children respectful behavior, as well as how to spot disrespectful tendencies. You also should be aware of these behaviors.

Thoughts

Try and visit that person who has been sentenced within your family. No matter how far it is. And bring the youngest member of your family with you as well.

The man who doesn't care for nor explains why he's not caring for his own kids, certainly will not care for you.

Never come between a man who's spending time with his family. Let that man see what you're doing, he'll respect you more.

Call a family member for no reason just to hear their voice and let them know exactly that. Waiting until they pass does no one any good.

Visit the beach and just sit and observe positive family interactions, as well as negative behaviors.

If you've identified that your surroundings have become too dangerous, MOVE. Your loyalty is to your health and the people living under your roof.

Be kindest to the people who depend on you. Their opinion of you should influence you the most.

Thoughts

Those who talk negatively about their family will eventually talk negatively about you, rephrased later.

Make it a family tradition each year to watch It's a Wonderful Life and The Ten Commandments; the family bonding moment will endure for all involved.

Do your part to promote your family values and people will respect you more.

We're not all wired to go to college, but as men, we have a biblical responsibility to care for our children.

Keep your family photo updated and share it with friends and other family members.

Be concerned with someone who doesn't have or is unwilling to share their family photo albums.

If your recently departed family member walked next to you all day, what would they say?

Thoughts

Send your mother a Hallmark card just because that says you love and miss her.

Know what it means to be a gentleman in the eyes of your mother... just ask her. If she's not around, ask your grandmother or any other elder female mentor.

Keep miniature chocolates at home. A home with chocolate is a happy home.

Do your best with your Christmas décor. It makes for a happy home during the holidays. Play Christmas carols and sing together as a family.

Your Christmas tree décor should be for those inside the home, not outside the home.

At years' end, reflect on what went right and what needs improvement.

Create an environment at home that makes your family love being home and want to stay home.

Question the home life of the ones who are never home or never want to leave you.

Thoughts

Help mend family conflicts only after hearing both sides of the story.

Identify what you love about your family or mentor and revert to that thought when a decision needs to be made. How will potential actions disappoint that person or will your decisions make them proud.

Choose family first. The mother of your baby is now your family.

Tommy at Breakfast

TOMMY AT BREAKFAST

Well, here's a little story I must share about two suited-up dudes you may recognize all too well. I was sitting at my local coffee shop enjoying an apple cinnamon pastry goodness, along with a large cup of black coffee and was trying not to be nosy, but couldn't help overhear a conversation from a table not quite two feet away. These guys must have had a cologne battle, because their scent overpowered the delicious aroma of my pastry and coffee. A couple of words or commonly repeated phrases that stuck with me from their conversation was "crazy whack-job liberals", "those people have no clue", and "liberals are ruining this country", on and on, you get the point. For 30 to 45 minutes, I was glued to their racist, Democrat-hating diatribe, and plus by now I had devoured my apple cinnamon goodness. My coffee, however, was still steaming and so was I at this point. They were openly speaking ill of people who didn't look like them nor vote like them. Feeling sick to my stomach, I left. Not only because I didn't want to go to jail that day, but my car was ready as well—I forgot to add that I was waiting for an oil change.

For the rest of the day, I couldn't shake it. Truly it doesn't matter what makes someone a liberal, a conservative, or an independent, yet being a racist is a separate concern. Why were they so easily ready to call someone out by their name or to speak of them so poorly? If you agree that we all have a right to our opinions, then shouldn't that right be respected. If we all thought the same way and had the same beliefs, would anything get done, would this be America?

So, these two dudes in suits agreed that liberals weren't only stupid and crazy, but also bad for America. Bad for America? Really? They were well-groomed, 30-something, BMW-driving, top public university students, Becky wife having, close-minded Americans. That's when it hit me. Yes, we may think differently, eat, drink, pray, love, and vote differently, but we're Americans first. Understanding that can help change your mind, help change political parties, even change your gender. However, one can't reverse time nor change one's birth city. Sure, citizen changes are completed daily for personal reasons. I'm sure, however, the fact that a person may identify with the country in which they currently live, doesn't change their feelings toward their birthplace. By now I'm sure you could've pictured what Tommy and Bill looked like and yep, you're right, down to the clear polished, manicured nails. I struggled with understanding why I didn't just interrupt their conversation. Was it a mind-my-own-damn-business thing, a know-my-roll-and-shut-my-mouth thing, or simply an I-don't-mind-because-they-don't-matter thing? Oh yes, as I stated earlier, it was the not wanting to go to jail thing. So, here's my conclusion. My brain can now create a should've, could've scenario, but in the end, Tommy has a right to say and do as he chooses. What he doesn't have the right to do is ruin the taste of my apple pastry goodness, with his dumbassery.

Friends

"You can choose your friends, but you can't choose family." This is such a true statement. With that said, choose your friends wisely. Surround yourself with those who love and support you. Spend time with those who make you feel great about you and allow you to be your true self. True friends will build you up and encourage you to be the best person possible. Jealous friends will tear you down and make you miserable along with them. Pay close attention to whom you open your heart.

Know which friends are there for good and those who are there for good times. Know which friend represents you and to whom.

Make a just the guys outing to a major sporting event. Know the difference between a friend and an acquaintance.

Be concerned about that guy who calls everyone Bro.

Know parent contact information for your friends. In case of an emergency, you'll be glad you have it.

Compete with your friends, not to beat them, but to motivate one another to do better.

As soon as you identify your lifelong friends, buy a video camera. You'll practice videotaping on these friends, so you'll be a pro by the time your kids come along. The memories of the good times will be priceless.

Hold your friends accountable for their actions, and they should hold you accountable for yours as well.

How would your friends react if the next time you met up, you weren't sagging and you told them you just enrolled in a technical trade course? Try it.

Thoughts

_____
_____
_____
_____
_____

Be the first to leave a party, the later the night goes, the more likely someone gets drunk and will say or do something that can't be unheard or unseen.

Invite your friends for dinner. Two days before the date, tell them that there's not going to be alcohol served at dinner. Then, the day before, tell them that you invited your parents as well, so you could spend more time with them. Make note of who still shows up to dinner.

Character

A person's character is defined by traits, quality, and high moral code. Decide early on how you'd like your character to define you. A person of high moral character is well respected in all aspects of life, opening doors to opportunities not afforded to all. You have full control over the character you choose, no matter your background. Achieving and maintaining strong moral character is probably one of the most important ways to achieve success in life.

Saying "I don't care," is the way the negative motivation gets satisfied at the completion or start of a poor decision.

Recognize that you don't know as much now as you will in 20 years. Think about this especially when heading to the tattoo shop.

Run to help the person in need yet know when to walk away.

Only drink when you're celebrating or when you're happy, never when sad.

Protest when you see injustice, protest with close friends, and/or family. Riots lose the message and give the opposition an excuse to discredit your message.

Hug tightly and appropriately yet be the first to let go.

If friends disrespect their family in front of you, then they'll disrespect your family behind your back.

Become an expert in conflict resolution, as well as keeping the peace.

Please, please, please, learn how to enjoy the silence all by yourself or with a friend.

Thoughts

_____

_____

_____

_____

_____

We, as a people, need to hold one other accountable for growth. What steps are you taking?

_____

Cry when it's appropriate, it's ok to let your loved ones see you cry.

_____

Memorize a romantic poem, a great quote, and a biblical verse.

_____

Be patient with people speaking English as a second language, chances are you're not that fluent in their native tongue.

_____

Learn the art of following directions by successfully completing a recipe in The Spirit of Christmas Cookbook.

_____

CHARACTER

Choose a life mate with a high moral character, keep a tight hold on spending habits, as well as a love for family and the church. You have the freedom to choose the order.

If someone needs help, then help them. Yep, it's as simple as that.

Once in your lifetime take a six-month, self-defense course.

Have self-control in all phases of your life.

Thoughts

Learn to play chess.

Excel in all things, if it's worth doing, it's worth mastering.

Help the lady with large objects into her car, but never into her home unless accompanied by another person.

Reach out to a mentor from past years, they'll be glad to know that you're doing well or they can offer guidance if you're not. At the end of the conversation, you'll both have benefited.

Look around and ask yourself: what do I need to do in order to be a better me? Then define a better you.

Refuse and reject the term Baby Daddy. Replace it with husband or dad. Providing for your creation is the essence of being a MAN.

Your favorite team's star player will never make you breakfast nor do your laundry, so don't put them ahead of the people who will.

Watch and appreciate the innocence of kids playing in the park. Observe the mistrust and judgmental eyes of the parents. You'll be amazed.

Argue, take a stand, make a point, and then shut up. The next person who speaks out of turn, loses. Focus on one point.

Thoughts

A bitch is a dog that barks and walks on four legs, with certain breeds having up to eight nipples. Our ladies are queens and should be treated as such. Let's know the difference between the two.

Return borrowed money or items before being asked to pay it back. You'll always benefit from having a good borrowing history with friends and family.

Reject the relationship with the person who throws their garbage in the streets and is too quick to curse.

Take accountability for your actions; with that said, ensure that the punishment fits the crime.

When donating, do it for yourself, as well as the cause. It's not important to broadcast your generosity.

Your activities at night have no bearing on your responsibilities for the next day. Transition. If you're going to party all night, make sure you're able to fulfill your responsibilities for the day, whether school, work, church, or picking someone up from the airport.

Keep those at a distance who consistently call you words other than your given name: dawg, bro, ni**a.

If you disrespect a lady don't get upset when someone disrespects your mom, sister, or female for whom you care.

Thoughts

A hoe is a gardening tool and bitch is a dog, don't forget it.

Understand the concept of paying it forward, then pay it forward.

If someone is where you want to be in life. Listen to their advice. When given sincerely, your result will be the same as theirs.

Enjoy people watching, then reflect upon about what someone else would think about your actions if they were watching you.

Grab a cup of coffee and watch the sunrise.

Pour a glass of really good whiskey and watch the sunset.

Try to find the beauty in everyone. If you can't, change your standard of beauty.

You can only be yourself. Many people become extensions of the friends, family, environment, and the music they listen to, so be true to yourself in all aspects of life and don't allow others nor situations to change the real you.

Keep your mind fed with positive influences, especially when you're surrounded by negativity.

Thoughts

Respect the passion of others. Many people live a lifetime without finding their passion.

Never be the one to say I told you so. Your advice will be taken more seriously the next time.

Study people, your environment, your future, and your past.

Always make mental notes of the way people react in situations involving you, as well as others.

Know when to spot a trend. If good decisions are consistent then so are bad ones.

Develop the necessary tools to assess risk.

Learn to be a good listener at all times and people will lie to you less often.

Stay away from stupid and selfish people, just listen and they'll prove themselves to be both.

Obey warning signs, they're there for a reason. For example: warning signs in health, environment, government issues, and relationships.

Thoughts

Choose three favorite words. Use them in a conversation with people you just met. Mine are: delightful, shenanigans, and exquisite.

You can call anyone bro, however, be selective as to whom you refer as a brother.

Wear cool socks, everyone will notice. However, only the truly confident will comment. Check out the sock collection of former president George H.W. Bush.

Learn how to iron your clothes using starch.

Undershirts are just that, to be worn under your shirt.

Don't rely solely on clothing labels. Wrinkle-free isn't always wrinkle-free.

Acknowledge a fellow brother with a nod and a slight point of the finger, a smile would be an additional friendly touch.

Thoughts

Satan My Friend

I'm stepping out tonight with my friend.

My friend who drives too fast, drinks, and steals anything any opportunity he has.

We all have that friend who can get the

best pills or smokes.

So, Satan comes in many forms.

Will I recognize him?

Last week my friend and I got in a car (yes, the same friend *DeRayl*) and went for a joy ride. We got it back in time. No one knew. The Lord was on our side. We'd been smoking weed in my friend's garage all week. No one's the wiser.

Man, God is good!

DeRayl picked me up during second period

and we partied all day.

We filled my Dad's bottle of whiskey with water and caramel-colored dye, as well as water in his vodka bottle. He's so smart!

He keeps my secrets of the illegal things we've done, yep that's my true brotha,

my ride-and-die, brotha.

My Dad tells me that there are friends of good, and friends for good times. You already know he's for good.

We caught a case some time back for stealing this pearl-white 5 series BMW, but his people were able to bail him out. Being slick, this ride-and-die dropped a dime and got off. At least that's the crazy story they told me. I took the rap and now I'm doing time. Last I heard his grandma took

him out and moved him to Atlanta.

He's so crazy, eight years have passed, and I can't wait to see my dawg. My other brotha we called Rainbow, said that DeRayl now owns two daycare franchises with his arrow straight cousin Dough Boy. He has three kids, married this trick Malarie, and lives in a three-bedroom house in the

Atlanta suburbs.

How did my ride-and-die do it? I know he didn't snitch, but I'm good. When I get in the free, I'm sure he'll hook a brotha up.

It'll be 10 years in March, but my P.O. told me not to call, that he's in Stone Mountain doing well, and his old lady isn't gonna let him see me.

Man, it's going to be like old times when I get out.

If I can only get him to answer his phone!!

Love and Romance

Who doesn't want a fairy tale romance at least once in their life? How one begins a relationship can define that relationship long term. Some are wonderful and healthy, while others can be co-dependent and challenging. Treat your significant other as you'd like your mother or father to be treated. "Love is patient, love is kind. It does not envy, it does not boast, it is not self-seeking." – 1 Corinthians 13:4

Before getting married or beginning to date, write down the top five qualities you'd want in a partner, excluding butt size. Be sure to include kindness.

Know your partner/girlfriend/wife's favorite chocolate, flower, and place to eat.

Take your partner to the theater, then out for dessert. The memory of that night will last a lifetime.

Once in a relationship, know your partner's expectations, their likes and dislikes, starting with a curfew.

For absolutely no reason, tell your partner how you feel about them. Say "I love you" and "I'm glad you've chosen me"—it seems corny, but your day will be much more relaxing and you'll feel better as well.

Know when to take the next step in a relationship. Conversely, know when to call it a day and move on.

Never cheat. The hurt is ongoing for your partner and IF they forgive you, you'll feel terrible in the good times for what you've put them through. The hurt endures on both ends.

Thoughts

_____
_____
_____
_____
_____

Decide early in a marriage who's responsible for what: vacation planning, paying bills, even upkeep of the interior, as well as exterior of the home.

Don't lie just to entice someone to sleep with you, the truth will come out eventually. That person might choose to exact revenge or try to get back at you, but then you'll call them crazy. Hell, they're crazy, because you began the relationship with a lie.

Identify the qualities you admire in your mother, if you're able to find these qualities overnight, you'll treat your current relationship better.

Watch Christmas movies with someone you love.

Insist on meeting your girlfriend's parents early in the relationship. Greet her father first. When leaving, say goodbye to the mother last.

Have patience when waiting for someone you care about to return home, at least you know they're coming home. When the impatient desire starts up, think about the alternative.

When a relationship breaks up, learn what you could have done better.

Never leave the person who possesses 80 percent of the characteristics for which you're looking, for the person who possesses only 20 percent of your preferred characteristics. You'll argue 80 percent more of the time.

Thoughts

_____
_____
_____
_____
_____

No one has 100 percent for which you're looking. If they say they do, then run! If you think they do, still run. When the true person is revealed, it will hurt deeply and your self-esteem will be crushed.

If your partner was fast to bed with you, they'll be fast to bed with someone else, so please don't kid yourself.

Get married and be committed. Commitment is the primary ingredient for every successful relationship.

In a relationship, being right is less important than listening to your partner.

When holding hands in the cold, take off your gloves. If cold, hold your partner's gloveless hand in your coat pocket. Your partner will always remember that moment.

Listen to the words your partner uses and look into their eyes while you're talking. Make this a habit and your relationship will grow stronger.

Don't buy the variety pack of anything; this is an argument waiting to happen undoubtedly since you both could like and dislike the same items.

Make it a practice to argue over a pint of ice cream... nuff said.

Thoughts

Be selective with whom you go to bed. Big booty Kim might be great for one night, but college student Jen is a better long-term investment.

If your partner isn't seeing your best, let them see it before you start to lose interest.

Only a strong woman can appreciate a strong man.

Finance

It's not necessarily how much money one earns in life that can make them financially secure, yet how one manages their money. Knowing how to budget in order to cover the cost of living in general, while saving for unexpected expenses, makes all the difference. Save first, treat yourself from time to time, but remain prudent and never overspend.

Treat your bank account with the accuracy of a surgeon's hand. Overdrafts are expensive and it damages your good name.

No matter how successful you become, never purchase a boat of any kind. If the urge takes you, rent the best one you can.

As with a boat, if you get the urge to buy a motorcycle, rent one first.

Have at least two lawyers on your cell phone that you know personally.

Know how to shop for health insurance, understand deductibles, HMO, PPO, and the different life insurance options.

Don't waste money. The average female slave sold for more than $350 in the late 1780s.

Whenever possible, support the black small business owner, especially a restaurant. Get to know the owners, they'll soon learn your favorite dish.

Be honest on your tax returns, the peace of mind of not being audited by the I.R.S is invaluable. Not owing the I.R.S. is priceless. You never want to know that feeling.

Thoughts

_____

_____

_____

_____

_____

If you must, borrow money from friends or family, yet try your best to never use a payday loan. Interest at pay off on a payday loan can be as much as 150 percent.

If you need to hide money, put it inside your favorite book, in your favorite chapter, then you'll never forget where it is.

Keep a minimum of $300 cash in your home.

Until you're well established financially, pack your lunch and eat out only once a week, preferably on Friday for dinner or lunch.

Start investing for your future early, your biggest wealth-building tool is your income, just ask Dave Ramsey. If you don't know of him, Google him.

Before supporting the local Scouting organization, research how the money is being spent.

Try not to set up an automatic draft until you're financially capable.

Thoughts

Don't write checks if you don't have the money to cover them. First, it's illegal. Second, you'll incur overdraft fees from the bank, in addition to fees from the company to which you wrote the check.

Choose quality over price, and always ask the reason why something is discounted.

Know the difference between cheap and inexpensive.

Collect reward points that never expire. If they do expire, make sure there's a cash-out option.

FINANCE

Learn how to use an investment calculator. One hundred dollars invested in the market in 2002 is now valued at more than $550 today. Do the math on the value of $100 invested every month since 2002.

Know how to read the stock ticker, along with market reports. Read market trends analysis and forecasting journals.

Thoughts

Loyalty

Love all things that you hold dear.

Own your thoughts and your actions.

Yours is what you own what motivates you, your actions are the causes that drive and inspire. Moving beyond what's purchased.

All things are obtainable with dedication, passion, and consistency. It's all you have to give in a relationship, oneself, or as an employee.

Legacy is as simple as what is said and left behind when you're gone, when you leave the room, or when you die.

Time is given to everyone. The use of time determines the path one takes—the most important commodity.

Yesterday's activities will either uphold or crumble all things designed for your good.

Food

Food nourishes the soul and brings people together. Family and friends gather in the kitchen and around the table to reconnect and bond. What we choose to put into our bodies will impact us long term, however, so treat your body as a sacred vessel. Life revolves around food: family gatherings, first dates, special events, support for one another . . . the list is endless. Bon Appétit!

Eat with your mouth closed, then check your teeth and breath afterward.

Eat slowly, since good food should be enjoyed. If you're not enjoying it, why eat it? If you don't have time for a good meal, enjoy a high-fiber bar.

Enjoy a toasted strawberry or other flavored cream cheese bagel.

Learn how to make good smoked ribs and chicken when friends are invited over, you'll always get positive reviews.

Buy organic vegetables. You'll taste the difference. Your body will show the difference.

When you stumble across an easy and delicious recipe, share it with your mother or grandmother first. The call will make their day.

Stay away from any beverage with drink in the name, this includes orange and grape drinks. You'll thank me when you're in your 50s and 60s.

Try different cuisines, it will broaden your perspective on other cultures. Believe me, try it. I bet you didn't always like broccoli or onions.

Thoughts

_____
_____
_____
_____
_____

Enjoy a good salad with grilled chicken, cranberries, and thinly sliced apples.

Own the most expensive rice cooker you can and use it often. It will pay for itself within three months.

A good seafood restaurant should have crab cakes and lobster bisque. If both are good, this would be a great spot for a first date, engagement, or anniversary.

Drink eight glasses of water and limit preservative intake from food and drink.

Try to limit food intake, you'll never get fat with one serving, you could, however, gain weight on the second and third servings.

Appreciate good health. Start off by staying away from greasy food.

Thoughts

Faith

Strong faith can get us through the worst of times and help us celebrate the best of times. Keeping faith strong is the key to helping us all navigate through life's most difficult circumstances. Faith brings family and friends together to worship God, strengthening relationships of all kinds. Stay true to yourself and your relationship with God. This is one of the most important things you can do for yourself, your family, as well as all those in your life.

Respect all religions, even ones you don't understand. Reflect on what separates your beliefs.

Know the Lord's Prayer and know how to say Grace in public. Always be prepared to say Grace when asked, never refuse the privilege.

Know that there's a jealous and just God. Your actions answer to a higher power.

Go to church every Sunday, not just on Easter and Christmas.

Be polite, quiet, well dressed, and respectful always, but especially at church, there's a good chance someone in the room knows your parents or at least knows someone important to you.

Know the Ten Commandments backward and forward.

Learn how to say Grace before eating. Make it one that you can recite for Thanksgiving dinner.

Thoughts

Get in agreement with God.

Go see your church's Christmas pageant.

Know This…

What's in a word, and how important are the words you're using? Do we own the cultural or regional definition of key social definitions or have we created our own?

Decency, morality, family, respect, standards, knowledge, consistency, and love. The ones who understand the true meaning of these words and have implemented them into their vocabulary are fortunate enough to be blessed. However, those who are described as such are the ones who have true discipline.

You can, may, and will think of other words for argument purposes, however, when you circle back to the ones who conquer their idea of success and fulfillment, these words will be at their core.

Government / World History

Ever hear the saying: History Repeats Itself? Knowing this should encourage you to become interested in history, if you're not already. Understanding the role of government, local, state, and federal, will help you understand how to use your voice and make positive change within your own community. Remember, every vote counts. It is a privilege and a responsibility to cast a vote. Don't complain about the current government if you didn't participate in voting!

If you must apply for government assistance, make sure you learn a trade while waiting for your next opportunity.

Know the history of the town in which you live, as well as the bio of the guys who carved the way.

Know someone in your local government by their first name, but never use it in public.

Learn the history of Haiti and you'll be surprised by how it shaped or could have shaped the United States.

Intimately understand the differences between the major political parties.

GOVERNMENT / WORLD HISTORY

Illegal activities will go on to be successful only for a short span.

Vote in primary elections yet pay even closer attention to the down-ballot candidates. They'll affect your community more directly.

Barack Obama demonstrated to us what can happen when we dream BIG. Yes, we can, is more than a catchphrase.

Thoughts

_____

_____

_____

_____

_____

While having a conversation with an old white man, ask how he viewed race when he was young? Also ask about his parent's view regarding race.

While having a conversation with an old black man, ask how he viewed race when he was young? Also ask about his parent's view regarding race.

Don't put credence in Black History month. Black history is American history, and we recognize American history year-round.

Respect black women, it's four times more difficult for them to succeed than white men. When you see a black woman just passing by, please show the utmost respect. They are the only segment of our population that was told that their natural hair was unprofessional.

GOVERNMENT / WORLD HISTORY

Develop a good understanding of the constitution. If confronted, never say a word without representation. "I'd like to speak with my lawyer" is the first, second, and third things you should say, if asked a third time. Repeat: "Are you denying me my constitutional rights?"

Once in your life, take a trip to the Birmingham Civil Rights Institute, National Civil Rights Museum, or The Charles H. Wright Museum of African American History. You'll think twice about disrespecting the black woman, as well as using the word nigger or nigga.

Thoughts

Download the U.S. Constitution and the King James Bible version app on your mobile device. Read while waiting in court, at a doctor's office, waiting on a friend, or in the hospital.

When given an opportunity show respect to our nation's veterans. Get involved with charity events created to help veterans. Wounded Warriors, Camp Hope, or Intrepid Fallen Heroes Fund. Also, always thank a veteran for their service when you see them in public.

Know the leading members of the Black Lives Matters chapter in your area.

Know when you're witnessing history in the making from Vance Scully to WikiLeaks to Donald Trump.

Be politically neutral, your boss may side with the other party.

Success

How do you define success? Each person has their own idea of what success means to them. To one it could be moving up the employment ladder, the amount money in the bank, or material items gathered. To others it could be strong relationships in life, academic goals, or giving back to others. Define your success and go for it with all your heart.

Whenever success reaches you, celebrate for one day, and move on. Far too often, you see people at 40 years of age replaying the successes of their teenage years.

Wake up each day with a plan. What is it that you need to do before 9 a.m.? How exactly are you holding yourself accountable? People with a plan rarely sleep past 8 a.m.

Define what success means to you: personally, spiritually, and professionally.

Dress the way you like to be treated. If you dress like a potential inmate, make sure you're able to offset an opinion by your conversations.

Winners win and performers perform. Both are successful people. Succeeding is simply a choice, on the other hand, so is losing.

Multiple-level marketing, no matter the product or pitch, doesn't work. Success is a result of working with your hands, as well as consistency.

Play fair yet play to win. Losers are the only ones comfortable with losing.

Thoughts

Your last name is important, it represents all who came before you and is your link to generations to come. Read the story of the namesake of Chicago's O'Hare International, one of the busiest airports in the country.

Set your standards for life and surround yourself with people of similar standards.

Find an exercise regimen that works best for you. Pick a specific day and create a schedule. Even no schedule is a type of schedule.

Before beginning any endeavor, assign a success-to-failure ratio. If that's not possible, consult with someone who already succeeded in that same area.

Read this book once a quarter or at least once a year. Give it to your friends, if you want them to remain your friends. You're not going to be able to fly like an eagle hanging with turkeys.

If you're not a champion, honestly record the reasons why. Set a timetable and start eliminating your barriers to success.

Refrain from being a jack-of-all-trades and master of none.

Thoughts

_____
_____
_____
_____
_____

Are you proud of the person you've become? If yes, great! If not, change.

Set your clock 10 minutes fast.

Set really high standards each year, incredibly high. Write down your plan. If you're barely successful in reaching your goal, you'd have a better year.

Quotes from the Heart

"Working hard is a term used by the observer since hard work is viewed by the participant."

Y.R. Spence

"Love first with eyes open and heart closed until there's a reason to close your eyes and open your heart."

Y.R. Spence

"Knowing who you are is important, being able to honestly respect that person is the end of your journey to true fulfillment."

Y.R. Spence

"Eighty percent of a healthy lifestyle is what you eat. Finding the match between nutritional value and taste bud excitement is the continuous challenge."

Y.R. Spence

Health & Hygiene

Good hygiene and a healthy body not only are extremely important to one's overall health, but to all those in one's life. A parent who cares for family must remain healthy in order to be available to them. Good hygiene helps keep one healthy and creates more social, as well as professional opportunities.

Fill prescriptions with your independent, good neighbor pharmacy to help keep the smaller pharmacies in business. The major chain stores won't miss you.

Don't waste water! Seventy-five percent of the world's population sees water as a needed commodity. Millions throughout the world die annually from lack of water resources.

Maintain good hygiene. Don't stink!

Keep your weight down and focus on a good credit score.

Don't take the risk of doing anything that can damage your knees or back.

Wear comfortable shoes.

Always be well-shaven and well-groomed. Only when you sign that million-dollar contract like your favorite rapper or athlete, can you then do as they do.

Learn how to cut your own hair.

Always brush your tongue while brushing your teeth as it helps combat bad breath.

Thoughts

_____
_____
_____
_____
_____

Take care of your young back and knees. Your 50-year-old self will thank you.

Treat the smallest health concerns with the greatest importance.

Stay current with all of your doctors' appointments. Be prepared with a minimum of five questions with each visit.

Know the process of admittance to the emergency room before you need it.

Know the signs of a drug user before it gets too far, the behavior of an addict is inconsistency.

You'll never admit to a gambling or drug problem, however, if you're told that you have a problem within a three-month period by several different people, well then there's a problem... seek help immediately!

If you smoke, STOP! Never let smoking become a nuisance for someone else. Above all, never smoke in your car.

Be sensitive to other people's allergies. Anyone can become allergic to anything at any stage in life.

Thoughts

Home Life

Nothing is more comforting than a harmonious home life. Any dwelling can be a home, whether a house, apartment, hotel, or tent. Home is where the heart is. One finds love, warmth, and happiness in a healthy home. Create a loving home environment, wherever you are and your soul will be content.

Be known for the cologne you use and the ice cream you like the most.

Own a dog, they'll always be there for you even when humans won't, plus they're better listeners.

Bathe your dog, the experience will deepen the love both of you share.

When taking your dog for a walk, always clean up their mess.

Buy a house where the air filters are easily accessible.

Take a home-decor class, focusing on a fall and winter theme, specifically Thanksgiving and Christmas.

Wipe your feet before entering a home and take your shoes off before being told. The show of respect will endure.

Make sure that the front entrance, kitchen, and bathrooms are always clean in your home.

Thoughts

Always keep a set of batteries in your home. Undoubtedly, you'll thank me at 10 p.m. when all stores are closed and your remote battery or flashlight is dead.

Keep the number of flashlights in one location equal to the number of people in the house, always make sure you have the biggest flashlight.

Learn how to paint your home interior. Your home will be forever changing and it's a great way to invite new colors into the home.

Always keep a brush, shoe polish, and travel kit in your home.

Turn off the lights when leaving a room.

Turn off the television after 10 p.m. unless you're watching "Saturday Night Live".

Keeping your home clean, isn't the responsibility of only one person. Happily do your part. Nothing beats this sense of accomplishment.

Thoughts

Develop a quiet space in your home. Your go-to thinking spot. This also can serve as the time-out corner.

Keep your garage clean, in addition to all top draws in the kitchen and glove compartment in the car.

Always use a calendar and keep it updated with important dates for yourself and those for whom you care.

Take a stroll through the countryside, these memories will be more appreciated as you get older.

Wear your team's jersey, not a player's jersey. The teams do things with you in mind. The player doesn't even know your name.

Give a pound or a dab to everyone until they've earned a handshake.

Pick up your high school yearbook and keep it in a safe place. Twenty years from now you'll value this book and the memories inside. If you don't enjoy it, you could always give it to someone who lost their yearbook along the way, making a friend for life.

Thoughts

Know when to appreciate life's special moments.

Stop and smell the drying paint, cars speeding by, the tick-tock sound of a clock, as well as all life's tiny blessings.

Sleep (not much more to add).

Carry a portable charger and make sure it's charged. Charge your phone at night.

Keep a good set of tools in your home. Spend money on a good screwdriver.

I'm a Proud Black Man

I call my wife by her name. I've never had to converse with a female dog. Unfortunately, I know not that language.

I put the extra 100 I saved in Home Depot stock, not on a round of Hennessy shots at the bar. I spend my money on the financial security of my family and not the latest shoe by Nike.

Yes, I'm a proud black man.

I live somewhere yet stay nowhere.

Yes, I'm a proud black man.

I welcome interrogation by the law, calmly and respectfully. Food for the family is more valued than ____, you fill in the blank. I reject the Baby Daddy adjective and welcome the term my baby's father.

Yes, I'm a proud black man.

I know the difference between a daddy and a father. I wouldn't disrespect the baby's daddy who tucks his kids in nightly with someone who doesn't know his kid's favorite color.

Yes, I'm a proud black man.

Knowing this begins once I'm awake and until the day is finished and I'm heading to bed.

I respect myself and the decisions I've made.

So, when things go wrong due to a poor decision on my part, I hold myself accountable.

When things go right, it's due to the activities of the people around me.

Yes, I'm a proud black man.

I control my world.

Yes, I'm a proud black man.

I'm the only one responsible for my family's future.

I take my kids into the voting booth to show them the process.

Yes, I'm a proud black man.

It's normal to be educated and articulate. It's normal to have a healthy bank account. It's normal to have two jobs. It's normal to be a socially respected and proud black man.

Yes, I'm a proud black man.

My wife is my world and when she gets crazy or upset, it's me, it's my actions that causes her angry behavior.

It's normal to not engage in illegal actives. It's normal to learn a trade. It's normal to stay and grow with your family.

Yes, I'm a strong, proud black man.

I provide for the safety and security of my family's future again and again.

Yes, I'm a proud black man.

My value is seen in the manner in which I choose my bloodline over friends. I speak to my parents with love and appreciation, knowing that they'll not always be here.

Be that proud black man, not with the reflection in the mirror, but your conversation with a stranger when no one's looking.

Travel

A well-traveled individual often has a more open mind to accept and understand life's diverse communities. Travel is the best form of education, exposing us to new foods, cultures, ideas, as well as bonds those traveling and experiencing together. Travel makes us more well-rounded and more tolerant of others. If you have the opportunity, travel to a country where your native language is not spoken. It is humbling and will make you much more tolerant of non-native speakers in your own country.

Travel often. Start visiting surrounding states. Alaska residents, visit anywhere in the U.S. Mainland.

During long road trips, never hesitate to pull over and take a nap when exhaustion hits. If you're going to do this, it's best to park at a police or fire station. You'll be able to sleep without worrying about your safety.

Driving fast isn't cool, it's a sign of immaturity. On the other hand, driving too slow reflects a lack of importance of where you're going.

Learn to drive a standard transmission automobile. Shifting from first gear all the way to fifth is a driving experience like no other.

TRAVEL

Visit your city's main museum.

When traveling and wearing a backpack, take it off and carry it ahead of you once you board a plane or train. Be respectful of other passengers by not knocking them with the backpack as you pass, plus it's dirty.

Try to visit the White House at least once in your lifetime.

Thoughts

Know where to go for a good run or walk.

When seated on a plane, resist the urge to take the window seat. Always take the aisle seat and your knees will thank you.

Also, when flying ask to be seated on an exit row on the plane since there's more room and often the last to be filled.

Always keep at least a quarter tank of gas in your car and your engine in the long term will be healthier.

Walk on the safer side of the street, stay away from trouble, allow your instincts to guide you.

Reject the temptation to put political bumper stickers on your car... okay, okay, don't put any bumper stickers at all on your car.

Be confident under the hood of a car.

Keep a concealed box in the back of the truck with a gas can and jumper cables.

Don't drive drunk, and if you have, never tell anyone. It's not something to brag about. Be wary of the person who tells you differently.

Thoughts

Entertainment

Music feeds the soul and nourishes the heart. How often do we rely on a specific song to lift our spirits. Entertainment comes in a multitude of forms and impacts us all in different ways. Absolutely make entertainment a part of your life, just respect the fact that each opinion of entertainment is different from our own and must be respected.

Use headphones in public. We don't all have the same musical taste.

Use social media to enhance your reputation, not to tear down others.

Be able to recite a conversation from a favorite movie. This will validate your favorite movie choice for others.

Buy a vintage record player and buy your five favorite albums, then listen to them regularly.

Find a song that reminds you of someone special, family good times, as well as life's bad times.

Begin Monday or Friday with "Oh Happy Day" by the Edwin Hawkins Singers or from Sister Act.

Create a Donnie McClurkin station on Pandora.

Thoughts

Listen to long-lasting music, whichever the genre. Learn the music of Motown, classic hip hop, country, rock 'n roll, and R&B, including music by Otis Redding, The Beatles, Bob Marley, Kenny G, Al Green, Big Daddy Kane, and LL Cool J.

Enjoy movie trailers.

Watch videos of military service members coming home.

Resist the temptation of posting videos on YouTube.

Experience a Black Friday campout for yourself at your favorite store at least once. When your kids go with you, it could become an annual routine.

Being a Man is Being a Dad

I'm aware that another day isn't promised.
So, I say goodbye with an *I love you* and a kiss.
I will do more than provide food and shelter.
I'll build a life by building a home.

Choosing to grow old with your mom,
by respecting the time we have, and the words I use.
Yes, I'm a provider, preacher, soldier, general, chef,
carpenter, plumber, storyteller, and philosopher.

You learn when I'm teaching race relations,
past and present. You, however, learn more
by my actions when not a word is spoken.

Without wanting to go, one day I won't be around. The good Lord will call me home. That will be the worst pain I'll ever cause you. When that moment comes,
know that then I'll always be with you.
In the natural world, I've completed the best job
a man can accept. Turning over years of lifelong knowledge,
wanted or rejected.

Never compromise your standards, work smart, and dream big. If your dreams are big enough, and you've prepared for it, success and riches will come in great abundance. You'll still be a success by accomplishing a third of your endeavors. Sometimes success is at the beginning of a task.

When it's all said and done, saying I love you dad, isn't redundant. Dad means the one I love and the one that loved me before he knew me. The one who shows me strength and is not afraid of showing weakness. The one who's in the next room, on the other end of the line. The one you turn to for... anything and everything.

Bible Verses

*T*op *10 Recognized Bible Verses in No Particular Order*

"Do nothing out of selfish ambition or vain conceit. Rather, in humility value others above yourselves, not looking to your own interests, but each of you to the interests of the others."

                             Philippians 2:3-4 New International Version (NIV)

"Listen, my son, to your father's instruction and do not forsake your mother's teaching."

                             Proverbs 1:8 New International Version (NIV)

"Where there is no vision, the people perish."

                             Proverbs 29:18 (NIV)

"Trust in the LORD with all your heart and lean not on your own understanding; in all your ways submit to him, and he will make your paths straight."

Proverbs 3:5-6 New International Version (NIV)

"Do not rebuke an older man harshly, but exhort him as if he were your father. Treat younger men as brothers, older women as mothers, and younger women as sisters, with absolute purity."

Matthew 26:41 New International Version (NIV)

"Watch and pray so that you will not fall into temptation. The spirit is willing, but the flesh is weak."
1 Timothy 5:1-2 New International Version (NIV)

"Flee the evil desires of youth and pursue righteousness, faith, love and peace, along with those who call on the Lord out of a pure heart. Don't have anything to do with foolish and stupid arguments, because you know they produce quarrels. And the Lord's servant must not be quarrelsome but must be kind to everyone, able to teach, not resentful."

                              2 Timothy 2:22-24 New International Version (NIV)

"Finally, brothers and sisters, whatever is true, whatever is noble, whatever is right, whatever is pure, whatever is lovely, whatever is admirable—if anything is excellent or praiseworthy—think about such things."

                                      Philippians 4:8 New International Version (NIV)

"I have been crucified with Christ and I no longer live, but Christ lives in me. The life I now live in the body, I live by faith in the Son of God, who loved me and gave himself for me. I do not set aside the grace of God, for if righteousness could be gained through the law, Christ died for nothing!"

Galatians 2:20-21 New International Version (NIV)

"Even youths grow tired and weary, and young men stumble and fall; but those who hope in the LORD will renew their strength. They will soar on wings like eagles; they will run and not grow weary, they will walk and not be faint."

Isaiah 40:30-31 New International Version (NIV)

"However, I consider my life worth nothing to me; my only aim is to finish the race and complete the task the Lord Jesus has given me—the task of testifying to the good news of God's grace."

Acts 20:24 New International Version (NIV)

"Those who live according to the flesh have their minds set on what the flesh desires; but those who live in accordance with the Spirit have their minds set on what the Spirit desires."

Romans 8:5 New International Version (NIV)

My Brother's Shot

ENTERTAINMENT

Our team just won the big game after years of struggling and now the celebration is underway. My brother, pick your poison: whiskey, vodka, tequila, it's your choice. It's on me. I'll buy *my brother's shot* this time, until the next big fight or game when our team takes it all.

I've been working at this plant for years. They offer good benefits, good retirement, and the pay is excellent. Well, send me your resume. This time it's *my brother's shot* to show what he can do. Now go run circles around those jokers. Show them what hard work looks like.

It's the west regionals and Duane has the tallest, most physical kid guarding him. This is the first time we've gone this far in the tournament and we're incredibly excited. With four seconds left and down by two, we steal the ball and race down the court. Two feet behind the three-point line and with .08 seconds left, Duane's silky-smooth jump, hung in the air for what seemed like an hour and a half. And then swish, nothing but nylon. We won the crowd in an uncontrollable frenzy. *My brother's shot* not only won us the game, but the championship.

The sirens are loud as hell, people running, some standing still, crying. What's happening? I have eight missed calls, and 14 text messages from people I've not spoken with in months. As I pull up closer to my home, I can see yellow tape on the side of my brightly lit driveway, still running is a privately owned ambulance truck. My wife hearing my car, runs out. They tried to kill my brother. *My brother's shot*. How did this happen? Was it a drive-by or was it a case of mistaken identity? Tell me it wasn't those who want to be a hero racist cop Calvin and those guys. Please tell me, and then the paramedic says: "I think he's going to make it."

I love you son! The way you speak and act shows the world whether or not you love me.

About the Author

For the last 30 years, Y.R. Spence has worked as a certified life and relationship consultant, helping individuals and businesses with financial, personal, and relationship growth. As a life coach, he has assisted hundreds of individuals restore broken relationships, as well as become a better version of themselves. Spence is the author of *My Brother's Shot: The Boy to Man Handbook for Navigating the Teen Years*. In addition to working as a life coach, Spence is the founder and president of Malian Investment Group LLC, which has holdings in tech start-ups and franchises.

Spence's background in cognitive behavioral therapy and rational emotive therapy has enabled him to become a sought-after coach in the Houston area. Spence's expertise in helping multimillion-dollar business owners increase their profit year after year, only adds to an already expansive resume. He has been married to his wife Patricia for the last 27 years. Together they have two children, Malkia and Sebastian, and a dog, Winnie. Spence is a true foodie. When he is not working with his clients, he enjoys boiled crawfish when in season and barbeque all the time. Both Spence and his wife are still on the quest for the ultimate crab cakes.

www.ingramcontent.com/pod-product-compliance
Lightning Source LLC
Chambersburg PA
CBHW071206070526
44584CB00019B/2939